40-Day Journey with Dietrich Bonhoeffer

40-DAY

Journey

WITH DIETRICH BONHOEFFER

40-Day Journey Series

Ron Klug, Editor

Augsburg Books
Minneapolis

40-DAY JOURNEY WITH DIETRICH BONHOEFFER

Cover image: Dietrich Bonhoeffer, August 1935. Photo © Gütersloher Verlagshaus, Gütersloh, in der Verlagsgruppe Random House GmbH, München.
Cover design: Laurie Ingram

Library of Congress Cataloging-in-Publication Data
Bonhoeffer, Dietrich, 1906-1945.
A 40-day journey with Dietrich Bonhoeffer / edited by Ron Klug.
    p. cm. — (The 40-day journey series)
ISBN 978-0-8066-5368-6 (alk. paper)
1. Spiritual life—Christianity. 2. Devotional literature. I. Klug, Ron.
II. Title. III. Title: Forty day journey with Dietrich Bonhoeffer.
  BV4501.3.B6625 2007
  242—dc22
            2007022963

CONTENTS

SERIES INTRODUCTION

Imagine spending forty days with a great spiritual guide who has both the wisdom and the experience to help you along the path of your own spiritual journey. Imagine being able to listen to and question spiritual guides from the past and the present. Imagine being, as it were, mentored by women and men who have made their own spiritual journey and have recorded the landmarks, detours, bumps in the road, potholes, and wayside rests that they encountered along the way—all to help others (like you) who must make their own journey.

The various volumes in Augsburg Books' *40-Day Journey Series* are all designed to do just that—to lead you where your mind and heart and spirit long to go. As Augustine once wrote: *"You have made us for yourself, O Lord, and our heart is restless until it rests in you."* The wisdom you will find in the pages of this series of books will give you the spiritual tools and direction to find that rest. But there is nothing quietistic in the spirituality you will find here. Those who would guide you on this journey have learned that the heart that rests in God is one that lives with deeper awareness, deeper creativity, deeper energy, and deeper passion and commitment to the things that matter to God.

An ancient Chinese proverb states the obvious: the journey of a thousand miles begins with the first step. In a deep sense, books in the *40-Day Journey Series* are first steps on a journey that will not end when the forty days are over. No one can take the first step (or any step) for you.

Imagine that you are on the banks of the Colorado River. You are here to go white-water rafting for the first time and your guide has just described the experience, telling you with graphic detail what to expect. It sounds both exciting and frightening. You long for the experience but are somewhat disturbed, anxious, uncertain in the face of the danger that promises to accompany you on the journey down the river. The guide gets into the raft. She will accompany you on the journey, *but she can't take the journey for you.* If you want to experience the wildness of the river, the raw beauty of the canyon, the camaraderie of adventurers, and the mystery of a certain oneness with nature (and nature's creator), then you've got to get in the boat.

This book in your hand is like that. It describes the journey, provides a "raft," and invites you to get in. Along with readings from your spiritual guide, you will find scripture to mediate on, questions to ponder, suggestions for personal journaling, guidance in prayer, and a prayer for the day. If done faithfully each day, you will find the wisdom and encouragement you need to integrate meaningful spiritual practices into your daily life. And when the 40-day journey is over it no longer will be the guide's description of the journey that stirs your longing for God but *your own experience* of the journey that grounds your faith and life and keeps you on the path.

I would encourage you to pick up other books in the series. There is only one destination, but many ways to get there. Not everything in every book will work for you (we are all unique), but in every book you will find much to help you discover your own path on the journey to the One in whom we all "live and move and have our being" (Acts 17:28).

May all be well with you on the journey.
Henry F. French, Series Editor

PREFACE

Dietrich Bonhoeffer was executed in a Nazi prison on April 9, 1945, for his role in a conspiracy to assassinate Adolf Hitler and bring the Second World War to an end. His involvement in the conspiracy was grounded in his conviction that discipleship to Jesus Christ required Christians to stand in solidarity with the oppressed by standing for and with the oppressed against the oppressor. His death was the final witness to his profound belief that obedience to Christ inevitably involves one in concrete and responsible action against evil on behalf of the victims of injustice.

Toward the end of his life, in a letter to a friend written from his prison cell, Bonhoeffer confessed: "What is bothering me most incessantly is the question what Christianity really is, or indeed, who Christ really is, for us today" (*Letters and Papers from Prison,* 279). It is—or should be—a perennial question.

Every generation of Christians must ask this question within the complex and concrete realities that provide the immediate context for their faith and life. This little book is a tool to help you do just that. Here you will be given the opportunity to reflect deeply on a selection of readings from *Discipleship* and *Life Together,* two of Bonhoeffer's most widely read books, readings that may well change the way you think about Christian life and faith.

As you reflect on these readings, however, keep in mind that Bonhoeffer was not interested in speculative or theoretical answers to the question, "who Christ really is for us today." The only answer that truly matters is a personal and communal answer that can be lived in the concrete present as a fulfill-ment of God's will for us. This, of course, requires risky and radical obedience to the One who said: "Why do you call me 'Lord, Lord' and not do what I tell you?" (Luke 6:46). Discipleship for Bonhoeffer "is nothing other than being bound to Jesus Christ alone" (*Discipleship,* 59).

Bonhoeffer saw that the gospel brings freedom to act on behalf of those who are abused, the victims of injustice, whether the abused one is another person *or one's self.* God's will for us is discerned through patient, attentive listening to the call of Jesus in community, in the world, and in the deepest needs of our own hearts. The freedom to say no to abuse, the freedom to resist injustice, the freedom to follow radically where Jesus leads are gifts of *costly grace.* In the exercise of this freedom, one participates in the reality of Christ, the self-disclosure of God. Indeed, for Bonhoeffer one never encounters God apart from the world, nor the world apart from God—for both come together in Jesus Christ. The disciple encounters the reality of God both in the immediacy of relationship with Jesus Christ and in following Jesus into concrete, responsible, ethical action on behalf of human need.

In Bonhoeffer you will find a bracing, challenging, totally unsentimental invitation to discipleship that makes a difference. The British essayist G. K. Chesterton once wrote: "The Christian ideal has not been tried and found wanting. It has been found difficult; and left untried." Bonhoeffer invites us to give it a try.

For Bonhoeffer, Christian faith was not meant to be at the periphery of life hidden behind the four walls of a church, and God was not to be relegated to the task of taking care of those things we don't seem able to take care of ourselves—sin and death, for example. As he wrote from prison:

> [God] must be recognized at the center of life, not when we are at the end of our resources; it is his will to be recognized in life, and not only when death comes; in health and vigor, and not only in suffering; in our activities, and not only in sin. (*Letters and Papers from Prison,* 312)

Bonhoeffer's conviction that God wants to be encountered at the very center of life, at those places where life happens, comes both from his encounter (through the Word) with God embodied in the life, teachings, and death of Jesus, and from his own experience of God encountered in risky, radical obedience to Jesus in the concrete realities of his own life.

You are about to begin a 40-day journey with Bonhoeffer that may well lead to your own deeper encounter with God "at the center of life." It will be challenging. It will also be rewarding.

How to Use this Book

Your 40-day journey with Dietrich Bonhoeffer gives you the opportunity to be mentored by one of the great spiritual writers and Christian leaders of the twentieth century. The purpose of the journey, however, is not just to gain "head knowledge" about Bonhoeffer. Rather, it is to begin living what you learn.

You will probably benefit most by fixing a special time of day in which to "meet with" your spiritual mentor. It is easier to maintain a spiritual practice if you do it regularly at the same time. For many people mornings, while the house is still quiet and before the busyness of the day begins, is a good time. Others will find that the noon hour or before bedtime serves well. We are all unique. Some of us are "morning people" and some of us are not. Do whatever works *for you* to maintain a regular meeting with Bonhoeffer. Write it into your calendar and do your best to keep your appointments.

It is best if you complete your 40-day journey in forty days. A deepening focus and intensity of experience will be the result. However, it is certainly better to complete the journey than to give it up because you can't get it done in forty days. Indeed, making it a 40- or 20-week journey may better fit your schedule and it just might be that spending a whole week or half a week reflecting on the reading, the scripture, and the prayers, and practicing what you are learning could be a powerfully transforming experience as well. Again, set a schedule that works for you, only be consistent.

Each day of the journey begins with a reading from Bonhoeffer. You will note that the readings, from day to day, build on each other and introduce you to key ideas in Bonhoeffer's understanding of Christian life and faith. Read each selection slowly, letting the words sink into your consciousness. You may want to read each selection two or three times before moving on, perhaps reading it out loud once.

Following the reading from Bonhoeffer, you will find the heading *Biblical Wisdom* and a brief passage from the Bible that relates directly to what Bonhoeffer has said. As with the selection from Bonhoeffer, read the biblical text slowly, letting the words sink into your consciousness.

Following the biblical reading, you will find the heading *Silence for Meditation.* Here you should take anywhere from five to twenty minutes meditating on the two readings. Begin by getting centered. Sit with your back straight, eyes closed, hands folded in your lap and breathe slowly and deeply. Remember that breath is a gift of God; it is God's gift of life. Do nothing for two or three minutes other than simply observe your breath. Focus your awareness on the end of your nose. Feel the breath enter through your nostrils and leave through your nostrils.

Once you feel your mind and spirit settling down, open your eyes and read the Bonhoeffer text and the biblical text again. Read them slowly, focus on each word or phrase, savor them, and explore their possible meanings and implications. At the end of each day you will find a blank space with the heading *Notes.* As you meditate on the readings, jot down any insights that occur to you. Do the readings raise any questions for you? Write them down. Do the readings suggest anything you should do? Write them down.

Then move on to *Questions to Ponder,* where you will find a few pointed questions on the reading from Bonhoeffer. All along, keep in mind that the *Questions to Ponder* and *Journal Reflection* exercises are meant to assist you in reflecting on the Bonhoeffer and Scripture quotations. Stay at it as long as it feels useful, and do not feel that you have to answer every question. You may, instead, choose which questions or exercises are most helpful to you, realizing that these are general questions intended for all Christians and communities of faith. Think them through and write your answers (and the implications of your answers for your own life of faith and for your community of faith) in the *Notes* section. Sometimes a perfectly appropriate response to a question is, "I don't know" or "I'm not sure what I think about that." The important thing is to record your own thoughts and questions. When your mind is ready to move on, close your eyes and observe your breath for a minute or so.

Then return to the book and the next heading: *Psalm Fragment.* Bonhoeffer loved the psalms. He called them the prayer book of the Bible and encouraged their use for both personal and communal devotion. The *Psalm Fragment* is a brief passage from one of the Psalms that relates to what you have already read. Again, read it slowly and savor the words. It may give you another perspective on the day's readings and help unpack their meaning further.

Then move on to the heading *Journal Reflections.* Several suggestions for journaling are given that apply the readings to your own personal experience. It is in journaling that the "day" reaches its climax and the potential for transformative change is greatest. It would be best to buy a separate journal rather than use the *Notes* section of the book. For a journal you can use a spiral-bound or ring-bound notebook or one of the hardcover journal books sold in stationery stores. Below are some suggestions for how to keep a journal. For now, let's go back to the 40-day journey book.

After *Journal Reflections*, you will find two more headings. The first is *Intercessions*. Bonhoeffer was convinced that one of the highest services a Christian can perform is intercessory prayer for family and friends, for one's community of faith, for the victims of injustice, and for one's enemies. Under this heading you will find suggestions for intercessory prayer that relate to the key points in the day's readings. The last heading (before *Notes*) is *Prayer for Today*, a one line prayer to end your "appointment" with Bonhoeffer, and to be prayed from time to time throughout the day.

HINTS ON KEEPING A JOURNAL

A journal is a very helpful tool. Keeping a journal is a form of meditation, a profound way of getting to know yourself—and God—more deeply. Although you could read your 40-day journey book and reflect on it "in your head," writing can help you focus your thoughts, clarify your thinking, and keep a record of your insights, questions, and prayers. Writing is generative: it enables you to have thoughts you would not otherwise have had.

A FEW HINTS FOR JOURNALING

1. Write in your journal with grace. Don't get stuck in trying to do it perfectly. Just write freely. Don't worry about literary style, spelling, or grammar. Your goal is simply to generate thoughts pertinent to your own life and get them down on paper.
2. You may want to begin and end your journaling with prayer. Ask for the guidance and wisdom of the Spirit (and thank God for that guidance and wisdom when you are done).
3. If your journaling takes you in directions that go beyond the journaling questions in your 40-day book, go there. Let the questions encourage, not limit, your writing.
4. Respond honestly. Don't write what you think you're supposed to believe. Write down what you really do believe, in so far as you can identify that. If you don't know, or are not sure, or if you have questions, record those. Questions are often openings to spiritual growth.
5. Carry your 40-day book and journal around with you every day during your journey (only keep them safe from prying eyes). The 40-day journey process is an intense experience that doesn't stop when you close the book. Your mind and heart and spirit will be engaged all day,

and it will be helpful to have your book and journal handy to take notes or make new entries as they occur to you.

JOURNEYING WITH OTHERS

You can use your 40-day book with another person, a spiritual friend, or partner, or with a small group. It would be best for each person first do his or her own reading, reflection, and writing in solitude. Then when you come together, share the insights you have gained from your time alone. Your discussion will probably focus on the *Questions to Ponder;* however, if the relationship is intimate, you may feel comfortable sharing some of what you have written in your journal. No one, however, should ever be pressured to share anything in their journal if they are not comfortable doing so.

Remember that your goal is to learn from one another, not to argue, nor to prove that you are right and the other person wrong. Just practice listening and trying to understand why your partner, friend, or colleague thinks as he or she does.

Practicing intercessory prayer together, you will find, strengthens the spiritual bonds of those who take the journey. And as you all work to translate insight into action, sharing your experience with each other is a way of encouraging and guiding each other and provides the opportunity to correct each other gently if that becomes necessary.

CONTINUING THE JOURNEY

When the forty days (or forty weeks) are over, a milestone has been reached, but the journey needn't end. One goal of the 40-day series is to introduce you to a particular spiritual guide with the hope that, having whet your appetite, you will want to keep the journey going. At the end of the book are some suggestions for further reading that will take you deeper on your journey with your mentor.

Who was Dietrich Bonhoeffer?

Dietrich Bonhoeffer was one of the leading Christian theologians of the twentieth century, an ecumenical leader, and the author of spiritual classics like *Discipleship* and *Life Together*. A Lutheran pastor, he was a courageous leader against Hitler and the Nazis in Germany in the 1930s and 1940s. He worked to end World War II, defended and helped Jews, and became involved in a plot to overthrow Hitler. He was executed by the Nazis in 1945. His books are still widely read throughout the world.

Bonhoeffer was born in 1906 into a prominent German family. His father was a psychiatrist and university teacher of psychiatry. His mother was a religious woman who taught her eight children at home in their younger years. As a child, Dietrich Bonhoeffer showed a love of music and became an accomplished pianist. At home the Bonhoeffer family sang Bach cantatas.

By age seventeen Bonhoeffer was determined to study theology. After several years of study at the University of Tübingen, he served as an interim pastor in a congregation of German-speaking expatriates in Barcelona, Spain, where he was a popular preacher and especially loved by children and teenagers.

In 1930-31 he spent a year in the United States studying theology at Union Seminary in New York City. While there he regularly attended worship at African-American congregations in Harlem and came to love black spirituals.

Back in Germany he taught theology and became involved in ecumenical activities with church leaders in the United Kingdom and Scandinavia. He had hopes of traveling to India to learn from the Indian leader Gandhi but was prevented from that by the political situation in Germany.

In 1933 Adolph Hitler and the Nazi party took over control of Germany. They began to exert pressure against the Christian churches and the Jewish minority. In the ensuing "church struggle" between the government and the churches, Bonhoeffer played an increasingly vocal role.

In 1934 a group of Lutheran pastors organized in opposition to the state church controlled by the Nazis. This led to the formation of the Confessing Church, an independent Protestant church that resisted both the collaboration of the state church with the Nazi government and the racist nationalism of the Nazi movement.

Bonhoeffer led an opposition seminary at Finkenwalde on the Baltic Sea. It trained pastors for the so-called "Confessing Churches," which were in conflict with Hitler and the official state church. The Gestapo closed the seminary in 1937, but Bonhoeffer continued to train pastors illegally.

In 1939 Bonhoeffer spent the summer in New York teaching theology. Shortly before the outbreak of World War II, friends encouraged him to stay in America, but Bonhoeffer felt strongly that he needed to return to Germany to be part of the struggle there. He was recruited into the resistance in 1940. He and other conspirators hoped to overthrow the Hitler regime and make a negotiated peace with England and the other Allies.

In April 1943 Bonhoeffer was arrested. He spent the last two years of his life in prison. In April 1945 he was sentenced to death by Hitler and executed on April 9. His family did not learn of his death until they heard of a memorial service for him on BBC radio.

Beginning in the early 1930s, Bonhoeffer's books had been published in Germany. English translations began to appear in 1945. He became well-known especially for books like *Letters and Papers from Prison, Ethics, Discipleship* (first published as *The Cost of Discipleship*), and *Life Together*. He is now regarded as a major theologian and spiritual writer of our age.

40-DAY

Journey

WITH DIETRICH BONHOEFFER

Day 1

THOSE WHO FOLLOW JESUS' COMMANDMENT entirely, who let Jesus' yoke rest on them without resistance, will find the burden they must bear to be light. In the gentle pressure of this yoke they will receive the strength to walk the right path without becoming weary....Where will the call to discipleship lead those who follow it? What decisions and painful separations will it entail? We must take this question to him who alone knows the answer. Only Jesus Christ, who bids us follow him, knows where the path will lead. But we know that it will be a path full of mercy beyond measure. Discipleship is joy.

BIBLICAL WISDOM

Come to me, all who are weary and heavy laden, and I will give you rest. Take my yoke upon you, and learn from me; for I am gentle and humble of heart, and you will find rest for your soul. For my yoke is easy and my burden is light. Matthew 11:28–30

SILENCE FOR MEDITATION

QUESTIONS TO PONDER

- What is Jesus' "commandment" that we are to follow? (See John 15:12)
- If this commandment is Jesus' "yoke," how might we be changed if we bear it without resistance?
- Why might following Jesus' commandment lead to tough "decisions and painful separations"?

PSALM FRAGMENT

Make me to know your ways, O LORD;
  teach me your paths.
Lead me in your truth, and teach me,
  for you are the God of my salvation;
  for you I wait all day long. Psalm 25:4–5

JOURNAL REFLECTIONS

- To be a disciple is not just to believe in Jesus, it is to follow Jesus. In your journal, reflect on the ways in which you are presently following Jesus.
- Do you experience your discipleship as "joy"? Is the "burden" of your discipleship "light"?
- Do you sense there are places Jesus might want to lead you where you would rather not go? If so, where are they and what is holding you back?

INTERCESSIONS

Pray specifically for family, friends, and colleagues that they might clearly hear the call to discipleship (which is the call to love and justice), and that they might experience following Jesus' commandment as joy in the concrete realities of their lives.

PRAYER FOR TODAY

Lord Jesus, only you know where my path will lead, but I trust that, even if I do not know either the way or the destination, you are with me and before me, and I follow you with joy.

NOTES

Day 2

THERE ARE THREE THINGS FOR which the Christian needs a regular time alone during the day: *meditation on the Scripture, prayer,* and *intercession...*

In our meditation we read the text given to us on the strength of the promise that it has something quite personal to say to us for this day and for our standing as Christians—it is not only God's Word for the community of faith, but also God's Word for me personally.... We are reading the Word of God as God's Word for us. Therefore, we do not ask what this text has to say to other people. For those of us who are preachers that means we will not ask how we would preach or teach on this text, but what it has to say to us personally.

BIBLICAL WISDOM

Do not worry about anything, but in everything by prayer and supplication with thanksgiving let your requests be made known to God. And the peace of God, which surpasses all understanding, will guard your hearts and your minds in Christ Jesus. Philippians 4:6-7

SILENCE FOR MEDITATION

QUESTIONS TO PONDER

- Why are meditation on scripture, prayer, and intercession so important to the life of faith?
- What obstacles might stand in the way of taking time alone daily for meditation on scripture, prayer, and intercession? How might they be overcome?
- How might "reading the Word of God as God's Word for us," rather than as God's word for someone else, lead to spiritual transformation?

Psalm Fragment

How sweet are your words to my taste,
*   sweeter than honey to my mouth!*
Through your precepts I get understanding;
*   therefore I hate every false way.*
Your word is a lamp to my feet
*   and a light to my path.* Psalm 119:103–105

Journal Reflections

- In your journal reflect on your present experiences of prayer and meditation. Are they satisfying to you? Do you give enough time to these activities?
- How could you find more time in your daily life for meditation, prayer, and intercession?
- Write about something you've learned from meditating on scripture recently. How has it changed the way you are in your relationships or at work?

Intercessions

Pray for encouragement and wisdom for you, your family, and spiritual friends (name them) in reading God's Word. Pray for discernment in understanding and praying for the needs of others.

Prayer for Today

Lord, draw me to your living Word and let it be for me food for the journey.

Notes

Day 3

THIS ORDER AND DISCIPLINE MUST be sought and found in the morning prayer. It will stand the test at work. Prayer offered in early morning is decisive for the day. The wasted time we are ashamed of, the temptations we succumb to, the weakness and discouragement in our work, the disorder and lack of discipline in our thinking and in our dealings with other people—all these very frequently have their cause in our neglect of morning prayer. The ordering and scheduling of our time will become more secure when it comes from prayer.

BIBLICAL WISDOM

In the morning, while it was still very dark, he got up and went out to a deserted place, and there he prayed. Mark 1:35

SILENCE FOR MEDITATION

QUESTIONS TO PONDER

- In what ways might "prayer offered in the morning" be "decisive for the day"?
- Do you agree that many of the problems we encounter have "their cause in our neglect of morning prayer"? Why, or why not?
- How can prayer lead to the "ordering and scheduling of our time"?

Psalm Fragment

Give ear to my words, O LORD;
give heed to my sighing.
Listen to the sound of my cry,
my King and my God,
for to you I pray.
O LORD, in the morning you hear my voice;
in the morning I plead my case to you, and watch. Psalm 5:1-3

Journal Reflections

- Write about how you usually spend your mornings. What do you do before work or school?
- Are you satisfied with the way you spend your mornings? If not, how would you like to spend your mornings?
- How is prayer presently a part of your morning? Any changes you would like to make?

Prayer for Today

Lord, show me a time in the morning when I can listen to you for the day ahead and when I can talk to you for the day ahead.

Notes

Journey

Day 4

AFTER THE FIRST MORNING HOUR [of prayer], the Christian's day until evening belongs to *work*. "People go out to their work and to their labor until the evening" (Ps. 104:23). In most cases a community of Christians living together will separate for the duration of the working hours. Praying and working are two different things. Prayer should not be hindered by work, but neither should work be hindered by prayer. Just as it was God's will that human beings should work six days and rest and celebrate before the face of God on the seventh, so it is also God's will that every day should be marked for the Christian both by prayer and work. Prayer also requires its own time. But the longest part of the day belongs to work. The inseparable unity of both will become clear when work and prayer each receives its own undivided due.

BIBLICAL WISDOM

Whatever your task, put yourselves into it, as done for the Lord and not for your masters, since you know that from the Lord you will receive the inheritance as your reward; you serve the Lord Christ. Colossians 3:23

SILENCE FOR MEDITATION

QUESTIONS TO PONDER

- In what ways might prayer be hindered by work?
- In what ways might work be hindered by prayer?
- How are prayer and work related to each other?

Psalm Fragment

Let the favor of the Lord our God be upon us,
and prosper for us the work of our hands—
O prosper the work of our hands! Psalm 90:17

Journal Reflections

- Reflect on the work you do. Is it satisfying and meaningful? Is it work that reflects your values? Is it work that reflects your faith? Explain.
- In what ways does prayer support you in your work? In what ways does prayer help to shape your work and the way you do it?
- Besides the work you do for income, what other kinds of meaningful work do you do at home or in the community? How does prayer relate to that work?

Intercessions

Pray for your co-workers, that they might find real satisfaction and meaning in their work. Pray for your workplace relationships, particularly those where there may be conflict and tension. Pray that you and your co-workers would be mutually supportive and encouraging.

Prayer for Today

Lord, when I go out to work may I go joyfully and with enthusiasm for the tasks at hand. May my work be good for me and good for others.

Notes

THANKFULNESS WORKS IN THE CHRISTIAN community as it usually does in the Christian life. Only those who give thanks for the little things receive the great things as well. We prevent God from giving us the great spiritual gifts prepared for us because we do not give thanks for daily gifts. We think that we should not be satisfied with the small measure of spiritual knowledge, experience, and love that has been given to us, and that we must constantly be seeking the great gifts. Then we complain that we lack the deep certainty, the strong faith, and the rich experiences that God has given to other Christians, and we consider these complaints to be pious. We pray for the big things and forget to give thanks for the small (and yet really not so small!) gifts we receive daily. How can God entrust great things to those who will not gratefully receive the little things from God's hand?

BIBLICAL WISDOM

You will say in that day: I will give thanks to you, O LORD, for though you were angry with me, your anger turned away, and you comforted me. Surely God is my salvation; I will trust, and will not be afraid, for the LORD GOD is my strength and my might; he has become my salvation. With joy you will draw water from the wells of salvation. And you will say in that day: Give thanks to the LORD, call on his name.... Isaiah 12:1-4

SILENCE FOR MEDITATION

QUESTIONS TO PONDER

- What are the cultural forces in our society that work against the experience and expression of thankfulness?
- What are the "small gifts" we receive from God each day?
- How could such "small gifts" be affirmed, honored, and celebrated in a community of faith?

Psalm Fragment

Bless the LORD, O my soul,
* and all that is within me,*
* bless his holy name.*
Bless the LORD, O my soul,
* and do not forget all his benefits—*
* who forgives all your iniquity,*
* who heals all your diseases,*
* who redeems your life from the Pit,*
* who crowns you with steadfast love and mercy,*
* who satisfies you with good as long as you live*
* so that your youth is renewed like the eagle's.* Psalm 103:1-5

Journal Reflections

- At the end of each remaining day in this 40-day journey, write in your journal a list of those things from that day for which you are grateful.
- Reflect on how the "small gifts" you receive from God shape your life and your relationships.

Intercessions

Pray that you would be a voice of thanksgiving in your family, among your friends and co-workers, and in your community of faith. Pray that your voice of thanksgiving would encourage others to give voice to the many things for which they are thankful.

Prayer for Today

Lord, open my eyes that I may see the giftedness of my life and let my life be a hymn of praise and thanksgiving.

Notes

Journey

Day 6

GOODS ARE GIVEN TO US to be used, but not to be stored away. Just as Israel in the desert received manna daily from God and did not have to worry about food and drink, and just as the manna which was stored from one day for another rotted, so should Jesus' disciples receive their share daily from God. But if they store it up as lasting treasure, they will spoil both the gift and themselves. The heart clings to collected treasure. Stored–up possessions get between me and God. Where my treasure is, there is my trust, my security, my comfort, my God. Treasure means idolatry.

But where is the boundary between the goods I am supposed to use and the treasure I am not supposed to have? If we turn the statement around and say, *What your heart clings to is your treasure*, then we have the answer. It can be a very modest treasure; it is not a question of size. Everything depends on the heart, on you. If I continue to ask how can I recognize what my heart clings to, again there is a clear and simple answer: everything which keeps you from loving God above all things, everything which gets between you and your obedience to Jesus is the treasure to which your heart clings.

BIBLICAL WISDOM

"Therefore do not worry, saying, 'What will we eat?' or 'What will we drink?' or 'What will we wear?' For it is the Gentiles who strive for all these things; and indeed your heavenly Father knows that you need all these things." Matthew 6:31-32

SILENCE FOR MEDITATION

Questions to Ponder

- In our consumerist, acquisitive culture, how can we know when enough is enough?
- If "treasure means idolatry," how might a community of faith both sanction and promote idolatry?
- If we "loved God above all things," how might our relationship to "all things" change?

Psalm Fragment

The eyes of all look to you,
  and you give them their food in due season.
You open your hand,
  satisfying the desire of every living thing.
The LORD is just in all his ways,
  and kind in all his doings.
The LORD is near to all who call on him,
  to all who call on him in truth. Psalm 145:18

Journal Reflections

- Reflect (as honestly as you can) upon your particular idolatries, on those things (or people) to which your heart clings in such a way that they get between you and your obedience to Jesus.
- Wonder in your journal about what you might do to turn your heart from such idols to God.

Intercessions

Pray that you, your family, and friends (name them) might have the wisdom to identify your idols and the grace to let them go and love God above all things.

Prayer for Today

Lord, may my true treasure be knowing you and following you. May nothing stand in the way of your love for me and my love for you.

Notes

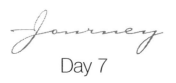

Day 7

DO NOT WORRY! EARTHLY GOODS deceive the human heart into believing that they give it security and freedom from worry. But in truth, they are what cause anxiety. The heart which clings to goods receives with them the choking burden of worry. Worry collects treasures, and treasures produce more worries. We desire to secure our lives with earthly goods; we want our worrying to make us worry-free, but the truth is the opposite. The chains which bind us to earthly goods, the clutches which hold the goods tight, are themselves worries.

Abuse of earthly goods consists of using them as a security for the next day. Worry is always directed toward tomorrow. But the goods are intended only for today in the strictest sense. It is our securing things for tomorrow which makes us so insecure today. It is enough that each day should have its own troubles. Only those who put tomorrow completely into God's hand and receive fully today what they need for their lives are really secure. Receiving daily liberates me from tomorrow.

BIBLICAL WISDOM

"But strive first for the kingdom of God and his righteousness, and all these things will be given to you as well. So do not worry about tomorrow, for tomorrow will bring worries of its own. Today's trouble is enough for today." Matthew 6:33-34

SILENCE FOR MEDITATION

QUESTIONS TO PONDER

- If "worry collects treasures, and treasures produce more worries," how might one stop worrying?
- How can we tell the difference between what we really "need" for our lives and what we think we need but really only want? Can we be content with what we really need?

- Practically speaking, what would it mean to stop our "abuse of earthly goods" and "put tomorrow completely into God's hand"?

PSALM FRAGMENT

How precious is your steadfast love, O God!
All people may take refuge in the shadow of your wings.
They feast on the abundance of your house,
and you give them drink from the river of your delights.
For with you is the fountain of life;
in your light we see light. Psalm 36:7-9

JOURNAL REFLECTIONS

- Write down your worries of today.
- Reflect on why you have these worries.
- How many of them have to do with things you have or want to have?
- Explore ways in which trusting God for today and tomorrow might relieve your worry and fear.

INTERCESSIONS

Pray for the people you know who are worried or afraid. Ask God to deliver them from their worries by increasing their trust in God's providential care.

PRAYER FOR TODAY

Lord, I place my worries in your gracious hand and live this day trusting that you are with me and that what I have is more than I need.

NOTES

Day 8

THE DISCIPLES ARE NEEDY IN every way. They are simply "poor" (Luke 6:20). They have no security, no property to call their own, no piece of earth they could call their home, no earthly community to which they might fully belong. But they also have neither spiritual power of their own, nor experience or knowledge they can refer to and which could comfort them. For his sake they have lost all that. When they followed him, they lost themselves and everything else which could have made them rich. Now they are so poor, so inexperienced, so foolish that they cannot hope for anything except him who called them.

BIBLICAL WISDOM

"Blessed are the poor in spirit, for theirs is the kingdom of heaven." Matthew 5:3

SILENCE FOR MEDITATION

QUESTIONS TO PONDER

- What kinds of poverty are there?
- In the life of faith, what is the point of disciples being poor?
- Bonhoeffer asserts that for Jesus' sake disciples lose everything. Why would Jesus want that?

Psalm Fragment

As for me, I am poor and needy,
*   but the Lord takes thought for me.*
You are my help and my deliverer;
*   do not delay, O my God.* Psalm 40:17

Journal Reflections

- Reflect on why you would (or would not) consider yourself poor as a disciple of Jesus.
- Could you imagine yourself as ever seeing poverty as a gift? Why, or why not?

Intercessions

Pray for the "rich" that they may have compassion for the "poor." Pray for the "poor" that they may have compassion for the "rich."

Prayer for Today

Lord, help me to lose everything for your sake and so discover all that I have and am in you.

Notes

EVERY ADDITIONAL BEATITUDE DEEPENS THE breach between the disciples and the people. The disciples' call becomes more and more visible. Those who mourn are those who are prepared to renounce and live without everything the world calls *happiness and peace.* They are those who cannot be brought into accord with the world, who cannot conform to the world. They mourn over the world, its guilt, its fate, and its happiness…. No one understands people better than Jesus' community. No one loves people more than Jesus' disciples—that is why they stand apart, why they mourn; it is meaningful and lovely that Luther translates the Greek word for what is blessed with "to bear suffering." The important part is the bearing. The community of disciples does not shake off suffering, as if they had nothing to do with it. Instead they bear it. In doing so, they give witness to their connection with the people around them. At the same time this indicates that they do not arbitrarily seek suffering, that they do not withdraw into willful contempt for the world. Instead, they bear what is laid upon them and what happens to them in discipleship for the sake of Jesus Christ. Finally, disciples will not be weakened by suffering, worn down, and embittered until they are broken. Instead, they bear suffering, by the power of him who supports them. The disciples bear the suffering laid on them only by the power of him who bears all suffering on the cross. As bearers of suffering, they stand in communion with the Crucified. They stand as strangers in the power of him who was so alien to the world that it crucified him.

~

BIBLICAL WISDOM

"Blessed are those who mourn, for they will be comforted." Matthew 5:4

SILENCE FOR MEDITATION

QUESTIONS TO PONDER

- Practically speaking, what does it mean to "mourn over the world"?
- How can a "community of disciples" bear suffering in a way that is healthy and redemptive?

- How can individual Christians and communities of faith not be conformed to the world and yet not hold the world in contempt?
- As Christians bear suffering for the sake of the world, how do they engage "the power of him who bears all suffering on the cross"?

PSALM FRAGMENT

You have turned my mourning into dancing;
*   you have taken off my sackcloth*
*   and clothed me with joy,*
*   so that my soul may praise you and not be silent.*
O LORD my God, I will give thanks to you forever. Psalm 30:11-12

JOURNAL REFLECTIONS

- List the times when you have mourned "over the world."
- Reflect on your experience of such mourning. What was it like? What did you do? How did you feel? What resources helped you live through your mourning?
- Have you ever had to bear suffering because of your Christian faith? Write about the experience. What did you learn from the experience?

INTERCESSIONS

Pray for world, "its guilt, its fate, and its happiness." Pray for those who suffer from the world's injustice, that they may find justice. Pray for the unjust, that they might experience repentance, find forgiveness, be filled with compassion, and begin to do justice.

PRAYER FOR TODAY

Lord Jesus, give me such compassion and love for our hurting world that I might truly mourn for all who suffer in any way.

NOTES

Day 10

NO RIGHTS THEY MIGHT CLAIM protect this community of strangers in the world. Nor do they claim any such rights, for they are the meek, who *renounce all rights of their own* for the sake of Jesus Christ. When they are berated, they are quiet. When violence is done to them, they endure it. When they are cast out, they yield. They do not sue for their rights; they do not make a scene when injustice is done to them. They do not want rights of their own.... But Jesus says, they will inherit the earth. The earth belongs to those who are without rights and power. Those who now possess the earth with violence and injustice will lose it, and those who renounce it here, who were meek unto the cross, will rule over the new earth.

BIBLICAL WISDOM

"Blessed are the meek, for they will inherit the earth." Matthew 5:5

SILENCE FOR MEDITATION

QUESTIONS TO PONDER

- What does it mean to say that disciples *"renounce all rights of their own* for the sake of Jesus Christ"?
- Why would disciples "not want rights of their own"?
- Should followers of Jesus be non-violent in their response to evil?
- In what sense can it be said that: "The earth belongs to those who are without rights and power"?

Psalm Fragment

O Lord, you will hear the desire of the meek;
*   you will strengthen their heart, you will incline your ear*
*   to do justice for the orphan and the oppressed,*
*   so that those from earth may strike terror no more.* Psalm 10:17-18

Journal Reflections

- Are there any rights that you would rather defend than "renounce…for the sake of Jesus Christ"? Explain.
- Think of the way you do life and live in relationships. Would you call yourself meek? Why, or why not?
- Is there a situation in your life now where you need the gift of meekness? If so, write about it. What might be different in that situation if you were truly meek? What do you need to do?

Intercessions

Pray for the powerful, the arrogant, those who clamor most for their own rights, that they might become truly meek and seek the good of others rather than their own good.

Prayer for Today

Lord Jesus, help me to renounce my own rights for your sake. Give me the gift of meekness and make me an "instrument of your peace."

Notes

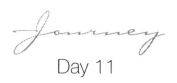

Day 11

DISCIPLES LIVE WITH NOT ONLY renouncing their own rights, but even *renouncing their own righteousness.* They get no credit themselves for what they do and sacrifice.

The only righteousness they can have is in hungering and thirsting for it. They will have neither their own righteousness nor God's righteousness on earth. At all times they look forward to God's future righteousness, but they cannot bring it about by themselves. Those who follow Jesus will be hungry and thirsty along the way. They are filled with longing for forgiveness of all sins and for complete renewal; they long for the renewal of the earth and for God's perfect justice.

BIBLICAL WISDOM

"Blessed are those who hunger and thirst for righteousness, for they will be filled." Matthew 5:6

SILENCE FOR MEDITATION

QUESTIONS TO PONDER

- What could it mean to renounce your own righteousness?
- Why do disciples "have neither their own righteousness nor God's righteousness on earth"? Is that a reason for pessimism or cynicism?
- If a church renounced its own righteousness, what changes might take place in the way that church relates to other churches, the secular world, and other religions?
- Would being always hungry and thirsty for righteousness lead to action or inaction? Why?

Psalm Fragment

For the word of the Lord is upright,
and all his work is done in faithfulness.
He loves righteousness and justice;
the earth is full of the steadfast love of the Lord. Psalm 33:4-5

Journal Reflections

- In what ways do you experience hungering and thirsting for righteousness in your own life? What could you do to alleviate that hunger and thirst?
- In what ways do you see our world hungering and thirsting for righteousness? What could your community of faith do to alleviate that hunger and thirst?

Intercessions

Think of those places and situations in our world where people suffer from unrighteousness. Pray that people of faith would say no to the suffering, no to the injustice, and then stand and work in solidarity with those who suffer "for righteousness."

Prayer for Today

Lord, may your righteous kingdom come in my life and in the world.

Notes

Journey

Day 12

THESE PEOPLE WITHOUT POSSESSIONS, THESE strangers, these power-less, these sinners, these followers of Jesus live with him now also in the *renunciation of their own dignity*, for they are merciful. As if their own need and lack were not enough, they share in other people's need, debasement, and guilt. They have an irresistible love for the lowly, the sick, for those who are in misery, for those who are demeaned and abased, for those who suffer injustice and are rejected, for everyone in pain and anxiety. They seek out all those who have fallen into sin and guilt. No need is too great, no sin too dreadful for mercy to reach. The merciful give their own honor to those who have fallen into shame and take that shame unto themselves. They may be found in the company of tax collectors and sinners and willingly bear the shame of their fellow-ship. Disciples give away anyone's greatest possession, their own dignity and honor, and show mercy. They know only *one* dignity and honor, the mercy of their Lord, which is their only source of life.

~

BIBLICAL WISDOM

"Blessed are the merciful, for they will receive mercy." Matthew 5:7

SILENCE FOR MEDITATION

QUESTIONS TO PONDER

- Practically speaking, what does mercy look like? How do merciful people act?
- Why is "renunciation of their own dignity" necessary if disciples are to be truly merciful?
- How might a church renounce its own dignity in order to be merciful?
- How is Jesus our model for renouncing dignity in order to be merciful?
- Is there anyone beneath the disciples' mercy? Why, or why not?

Psalm Fragment

They rise in the darkness as a light for the upright;
*   they are gracious, merciful, and righteous.*
It is well with those who deal generously and lend,
*   who conduct their affairs with justice.* Psalm 112:4-5

Journal Reflections

- Write about a time when you extended mercy to someone. How did you feel?
- Write about a time when you withheld mercy. How did you feel?
- Reflect on the ways in which God is merciful to you.

Intercessions

Think of someone who needs to experience mercy. Pray for them in their need. Ask God what you might do to show them mercy.

Prayer for Today

Lord, may your infinite mercy to me enable me to be truly merciful to all others.

Notes

Day 13

WHO IS PURE IN HEART? Only those who have completely given their hearts to Jesus, so that he alone rules in them. Only those who do not stain their hearts with their own evil, but also not with their own good. A pure heart is the simple heart of a child, who does not know about good and evil, the heart of Adam before the fall, the heart in which the will of Jesus rules instead of one's own conscience.... A pure heart is pure of good and evil; it belongs entirely and undivided to Christ; it looks only to him, who goes on ahead. Those alone will see God who in this life have looked only to Jesus Christ, the Son of God. Their hearts are free of defiling images; they are not pulled back and forth by the various wishes and intentions of their own. Their hearts are fully absorbed in seeing God. They will see God whose hearts mirror the image of Jesus Christ.

BIBLICAL WISDOM

"Blessed are the pure in heart, for they will see God." Matthew 5:8

SILENCE FOR MEDITATION

QUESTIONS TO PONDER

- How is it possible to live in our complex world and still give your heart "completely" to Jesus?
- What does it mean to say that people can "stain their hearts...with their own good"?
- How would those whose "hearts mirror the image of Jesus Christ" relate to other people, both friends and strangers?

PSALM FRAGMENT

Who shall ascend the hill of the LORD?
And who shall stand in his holy place?
Those who have clean hands and pure hearts,
who do not lift up their souls to what is false,
and do not swear deceitfully.
They will receive blessing from the LORD,
and vindication from the God of their salvation. Psalm 24:3-5

JOURNAL REFLECTIONS

- Bonhoeffer wrote that: "A pure heart is the simple heart of a child…" Think back to when you were a child. How did you see things differently as a child than you do now as an adult?
- What, if any, are the "defiling images" that stand between you and the vision of God? How might you begin to cleanse your heart of them?
- What, if any, are your various "wishes and intentions" that pull you "back and forth" and prevent you from seeing God? How might you begin to become free of them?

INTERCESSIONS

Pray for all the children that you know (and then pray for all children) that they would be protected from the "defiling images" culture tries to entice them with.

PRAYER FOR TODAY

Lord, help me to will one thing: to belong entirely and undividedly to you.

NOTES

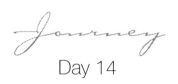

Day 14

JESUS' FOLLOWERS ARE CALLED TO peace. When Jesus called them, they found their peace. Jesus is their peace. Now they are not only to have peace, but they are to make peace. To do this they *renounce violence and strife*. Those things never help the cause of Christ. Christ's kingdom is a realm of peace, and those in Christ's community greet each other with a greeting of peace. Jesus' disciples maintain peace by choosing to suffer instead of causing others to suffer. They preserve community when others destroy it. They renounce self-assertion and are silent in the face of hatred and injustice. That is how they overcome evil with good. That is how they are makers of divine peace in a world of hatred and war.

BIBLICAL WISDOM

"Blessed are the peacemakers, for they will be called children of God." Matthew 5:9

SILENCE FOR MEDITATION

QUESTIONS TO PONDER

- What impact would it have on our culture of violence if individual Christians and churches were to *"renounce violence and strife"* as a mark of true discipleship?
- How might being "silent in the face of hatred and injustice" be compatible with non-violent resistance to evil?
- Why can violence never help the cause of Christ's kingdom?

PSALM FRAGMENT

Which of you desires life,
and covets many days to enjoy good?
Keep your tongue from evil,
and your lips from speaking deceit.
Depart from evil, and do good;
seek peace, and pursue it. Psalm 34:12-14

JOURNAL REFLECTIONS

- Have you ever thought deeply on the fact that your call to follow Jesus is a call to peace? Reflect in your journal on how that realization makes you feel. Any actions suggest themselves?
- Think of any people with whom you are in conflict or tension. Reflect on what might happen if the next time you met them you greeted them with a "greeting of peace."
- What experiences of peacemaking have you had? Reflect on what it felt like to be a peacemaker.

INTERCESSIONS

Pray for all politicians and government leaders that they might "renounce violence and strife" and embrace peacemaking as a priority at all levels of government.

PRAYER FOR TODAY

God of peace, you give me peace, now teach me to be a peacemaker.

NOTES

THIS DOES NOT REFER TO God's righteousness, but to suffering for the sake of a righteous cause, suffering because of the righteous judgment and action of Jesus' disciples. In judgment and action those who follow Jesus will be different from the world in renouncing their property, happiness, rights, righteousness, honor, and violence. They will be offensive to the world. That is why the disciples will be persecuted for righteousness' sake. Not recognition, but rejection will be their reward from the world for their word and deed. It is important that Jesus calls his disciples blessed, not only when they directly confess his name, but also when they suffer for a just cause.

BIBLICAL WISDOM

"Blessed are those who are persecuted for righteousness' sake, for theirs is the kingdom of heaven." Matthew 5:10

SILENCE FOR REFLECTION

QUESTIONS TO PONDER

- What do you think of Bonhoeffer's assertion that disciples *will be* "offensive to the world"?
- Why is it today that the world often seems more indifferent to Christians and the church than offended by them?
- In what way is a disciple "blessed" when he or she "suffers for a just cause"?

PSALM FRAGMENT

For the righteous will never be moved;
their will be remembered forever.
They are not afraid of evil tidings;
their hearts are firm, secure in the LORD.
Their hearts are steady, they will not be afraid;
in the end they will look in triumph on their foes.
They have distributed freely, they have given to the poor;
their righteousness endures forever.... Psalm 112:6-9

JOURNAL REFLECTIONS

- Write about a time when you suffered for doing the right thing. Reflect on your feelings about that experience.
- Have you ever held back from doing the right thing because you were afraid of rejection or suffering? If so, reflect on how it felt to hold back.

INTERCESSIONS

Think of people you know (or know of) who are suffering "for righteousness sake." Pray that they might receive courage and comfort from their faith and that they might prevail.

PRAYER FOR TODAY

Lord, give me the wisdom to know what is right and make me willing to suffer for a just cause.

NOTES

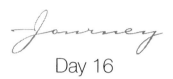

Day 16

"You are the salt"—not "You should be the salt"!
The disciples are given no choice whether they want to be salt or not. No appeal is made to them to become the salt of the earth. Rather they just are salt whether they want to be or not, by the power of the call which has reached them. You are the salt—not "you have the salt." It would diminish the meaning to equate the disciples' message with salt, as the reformers did. What is meant is their whole existence, to the extent that it is newly grounded in Christ's call to discipleship, that existence of which the Beatitudes speak. All those who follow Jesus' call to discipleship are made by that call to be the salt of the earth in their whole existence.

⌁

Biblical Wisdom

"You are the salt of the earth; but if salt has lost its taste, how can its saltiness be restored? It is no longer good for anything, but is thrown out and trampled under foot." Matthew 5:13

Silence for Meditation

Questions to Ponder

- What are the qualities of salt that make it an apt metaphor for Jesus' disciples?
- If Christ's call to discipleship changes our whole existence, in what ways should the disciple's life be different from those who have not heard or accepted the call?
- Is there any area of a disciple's life that is exempt from the call to be the salt of the earth? Explain.

Psalm Fragment

Give me understanding, that I may keep your law
*   and observe it with my whole heart.*
Lead me in the path of your commandments,
*   for I delight in it.*
Turn my heart to your decrees,
*   and not to selfish gain.*
Turn my eyes from looking at vanities;
*   give me life in your ways.* Psalm 119:34-37

Journal Reflections

- How does it feel to understand yourself as the salt of the earth?
- How salty are you?
- List the ways in which you are salt in your family, workplace, and community.

Intercessions

Think of places in your community where "salt" is needed. Pray for your community of faith that it may be up to the call to be salt in those places.

Prayer for Today

Lord, in response to your call, I want to be who you have made me, the salt of the earth.

Notes

M

Day 17

CHEAP GRACE IS THE MORTAL enemy of our church. Our struggle today is for costly grace.

Cheap grace means grace as bargain-basement goods, cut-rate forgiveness, cut-rate comfort, cut-rate sacraments; grace as the church's inexhaustible pantry, from which it is doled out by careless hands without hesitation or limit. It is grace without a price, without cost…

Cheap grace means grace as a doctrine, as principle, as system. It means forgiveness of sins as a general truth; it means God's love as merely a Christian idea of God. Those who affirm it have already had their sins forgiven. The church that teaches this doctrine of grace thereby conveys such grace upon itself. The world finds in this church a cheap cover-up for its sins, for which it shows no remorse and from which it has even less desire to be free. Cheap grace is, thus, denial of God's living Word, denial of the incarnation of the word of God.

Cheap grace means justification of sin but not of the sinner. Because grace alone does everything, everything can stay in its old ways. "Our action is in vain." The world remains world and we remain sinners "even in the best of lives." Thus, the Christian should live the same way the world does. In all things the Christian should go along with the world and not venture…to live a different life under grace from that under sin…

Cheap grace is that which we bestow on ourselves.

Cheap grace is preaching forgiveness without repentance; it is baptism without the discipline of community; it is the Lord's Supper without confession of sin; it is absolution without personal confession. Cheap grace is grace without discipleship, grace without the cross, grace without the living, incarnate Jesus Christ.

BIBLICAL WISDOM

What then? Should we sin because we are not under law but under grace? By no means! Do you not know that if you present yourselves to anyone as obedient slaves, you are slaves of the one whom you obey, either of sin, which leads to death, or of obedience, which leads to righteousness? But thanks be to God that you, having once been slaves of sin, have become obedient from the heart to the form of

teaching to which you were entrusted, and that you, having been set free from sin,
have become slaves of righteousness. Romans 6:15-18

Silence for Meditation

Questions to Ponder

- Why is it that the church so often proclaims and dispenses "cheap grace"?
- What happens to the "saltiness" of disciples in a church that "conveys such [cheap] grace upon itself"?
- What does it mean to say that cheap grace is "grace without the living, incarnate Jesus Christ"?

Psalm Fragment

Create in me a clean heart, O God,
and put a new and right spirit within me.
Do not cast me away from your presence,
and do not take your holy spirit from me.
Restore to me the joy of your salvation,
and sustain in me a willing spirit. Psalm 51:10-12

Journal Reflections

- In your journal make a list of all the characteristics of cheap grace that Bonhoeffer identifies.
- Do you find any of these characteristics in your own life or in the life of your community of faith? If so, reflect on them in your journal.

Intercessions

Think of the proclamation and practice of your community of faith and pray that they would be free of cheap grace.

Prayer for Today

Lord, you love me with an everlasting love. Deliver me from cheap grace that I may respond to your love with my whole life.

Notes

Day 18

THE WORD OF CHEAP GRACE has ruined more Christians than any commandment about works...

For integrity's sake someone has to speak up for those among us who confess that cheap grace has made them give up following Christ, and that ceasing to follow Christ has made them lose the knowledge of costly grace. Because we cannot deny that we no longer stand in true discipleship to Christ, while being members of a true-believing church with a pure doctrine of grace, but are no longer members of a church which follows Christ, we therefore have to try to understand grace and discipleship again in correct relationship to each other.

BIBLICAL WISDOM

What then are we to say? Should we continue to sin in order that grace may abound? By no means! How can we who died to sin go on living in it? Do you not know that all of us who have been baptized into Christ Jesus were baptized into his death? Therefore we have been buried with him by baptism into death, so that, just as Christ was raised from the dead to the glory of the Father, so we too might walk in newness of life. Romans 6:1-4

SILENCE FOR MEDITATION

QUESTIONS TO PONDER

- What do you think Bonhoeffer meant by saying: "The word of cheap grace has ruined more Christians than any commandment about works"?
- Why might cheap grace cause someone to give up following Christ?
- What is the correct relationship between grace and discipleship?

Psalm Fragment

Restore us, O Lord God of hosts;
*   let your face shine, that we may be saved.* Psalm 80:19

Journal Reflections

- Has the church's proclamation and practice of cheap grace ever led you to consider not following Christ anymore? If so, write about the experience.
- Do you know anyone who has given up following Christ because of cheap grace? If so, did anyone speak up for her or him?

Intercessions

Pray for the church, and for all Christians, that they may not succumb to the lure of cheap grace.

Prayer for Today

Lord Jesus Christ, I would follow you, no matter what the cost; lead me in the way of true discipleship.

Notes

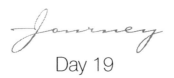

Day 19

COSTLY GRACE IS THE HIDDEN treasure in the field, for the sake of which people go and sell with joy everything they have. It is the costly pearl for whose price the merchant sells all that he has; it is Christ's sovereignty, for the sake of which you tear out an eye if it causes you to stumble. It is the call of Jesus Christ which causes a disciple to leave his nets and follow him.

Costly grace is the gospel which must be sought again and again, the gift which has to be asked for, the door at which one has to knock.

It is costly, because it calls to discipleship; it is grace, because it calls us to follow *Jesus Christ*. It is costly, because it costs people their lives; it is grace, because it thereby makes them live. It is costly, because it condemns sin; it is grace, because it justifies the sinner. Above all, grace is costly, because it was costly to God, because it cost God the life of God's Son—"you were bought with a price"—and because nothing can be cheap to us which is costly to God. Above all, it is grace because the life of God's Son was not too costly for God to give in order to make us live…

Grace is costly, because it forces people under the yoke of following Jesus Christ; it is grace when Jesus says, "My yoke is easy, and my burden is light" (Matthew 11:30).

BIBLICAL WISDOM

For you were bought with a price; therefore glorify God in your body. 1 Corinthians 6:20

SILENCE FOR MEDITATION

QUESTIONS TO PONDER

- If costly grace means that God wants things from us as well as for us, what might those things be?
- What is the difference between following Jesus Christ (costly grace) and simply believing things about Jesus Christ (cheap grace)?
- What does it mean to say grace is costly "because it costs people their lives"?

PSALM FRAGMENT

Glory in his holy name;
*   let the hearts of those who seek the LORD rejoice.*
Seek the LORD and his strength;
*   seek his presence continually.* Psalm 105:3-4

JOURNAL REFLECTIONS

- Have you experienced costly grace? If so, what did it feel like? If not, what do you imagine it might feel like?
- What would it mean for you to "leave [your] nets and follow him"?

INTERCESSIONS

Pray for the church and for all Christians, that they may proclaim and practice costly grace.

PRAYER FOR TODAY

Thank you, O God, for the costly grace you have offered me freely and which has made me a disciple of Jesus.

NOTES

Day 20

ONLY THE OBEDIENT BELIEVE. A concrete commandment has to be obeyed in order to come to believe. A first step of obedience has to be taken, so that faith does not become pious self-deception, cheap grace. The first step is crucial. It is qualitatively different from all others that follow. The first step of obedience has to lead Peter away from his nets and out of the boat; it has to lead the young man away from his wealth. Faith is possible only in this new state of existence created by obedience.

BIBLICAL WISDOM

As Jesus passed along the Sea of Galilee, he saw Simon and his brother Andrew casting a net into the sea—for they were fishermen. And Jesus said to them, "Follow me and I will make you fish for people." And immediately they left their nets and followed him. Mark 1:16-18

SILENCE FOR MEDITATION

QUESTIONS TO PONDER

- How do you understand the relationship between obedience and true faith?
- How might a "first step of obedience" change your relationship to Jesus?
- Why is the first step "qualitatively different from all others that follow"?

PSALM FRAGMENT

O come, let us worship and bow down,
*   let us kneel before the LORD, our Maker!*
For he is our God,
*   and we are the people of his pasture,*
*   and the sheep of his hand.*
O that today you would listen to his voice! Psalm 95:6-7

JOURNAL REFLECTIONS

- Is there a moment when you took a "first step of obedience"? If so, write about it. What was it like? How did it change your life?
- Do you need to take a "first step of obedience"? If so, any ideas or intuitions about what form that might take?

INTERCESSIONS

Pray that you, your family, and your spiritual friends would have the courage to be obedient to whatever God is calling you to.

PRAYER FOR TODAY

Gracious God, grant me the wisdom to see what you need me to do and the courage to do it.

NOTES

YOU COMPLAIN THAT YOU CANNOT believe? No one should be surprised that they cannot come to believe so long as, in deliberate disobedience, they flee or reject some aspect of Jesus' commandment. You do not want to subject some sinful passion, an enmity, a hope, your life plan, or your reason to Jesus' commandment? Do not be surprised that you do not receive the Holy Spirit, that you cannot pray, that your prayer for faith remains empty! Instead, go and be reconciled with your sister or brother; let go of the sin which keeps you captive; and you will be able to believe again! If you reject God's commanding word, you will not receive God's gracious word. How would you expect to find community while you intentionally withdraw from it at some point? The disobedient cannot believe; only the obedient believe.

BIBLICAL WISDOM

What good is it, my brothers and sisters, if you say that you have faith but do not have works? Can faith save you? If a brother or sister is naked and lacks daily food, and one of you says to them, "Go in peace; keep warm and eat your fill," and yet you do not supply their bodily needs, what is the good of that? So faith by itself, if it has no works, is dead. James 2:14-17

SILENCE FOR MEDITATION

QUESTIONS TO PONDER

- Jesus' commandment is that we love God who made us and that we love our neighbors as ourselves. How does obedience to this commandment nurture and nourish true faith?
- Why does rejecting "God's commanding word" keep us from receiving "God's gracious word"?
- What is it about rejecting God's commanding word that takes us out of community?

Psalm Fragment

Then they despised the pleasant land,
having no faith in his promise.
They grumbled in their tents,
and did not obey the voice of the Lord. Psalm 106:24-25

Journal Reflections

- Write in your journal about a practical experience of how your obedience to Jesus' commandment has nurtured and nourished your faith.
- Write about your experiences of Christian community. Reflect on both good and bad experiences. What is the difference between them?

Intercessions

Pray for your family and spiritual friends (and for all Christians) that they would continuously experience community grounded in love.

Prayer for Today

Lord, help me to see where I am rejecting some aspect of your will for me. Help me to obey and believe, believe and obey.

Notes

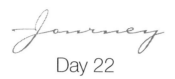

Day 22

THE MEASURE WITH WHICH GOD gives the gift of visible community is varied. Christians who live dispersed from one another are comforted by a brief visit of another Christian, a prayer together, and another Christian's blessing. Indeed, they are strengthened by letters written by the hand of other Christians. Paul's greetings in his letters written in his own hand were no doubt tokens of such community. Others are given the gift on Sundays of the community of the worship service. Still others have the privilege of living a Christian life in the community of their families.

BIBLICAL WISDOM

Now concerning love of the brothers and sisters, you do not need to have anyone write to you, for you yourselves have been taught by God to love one another, and indeed you do love all the brothers and sisters throughout Macedonia. 1 Thessalonians 4:9

SILENCE FOR MEDITATION

QUESTIONS TO PONDER

- Why is Christian community so important for the life of faith?
- What are the things that weaken community?
- What are the things that strengthen community?

Psalm Fragment

Worship the LORD with gladness;
come into his presence with singing.
Know that the LORD is God.
It is he that made us, and we are his;
we are his people, and the sheep of his pasture. Psalm 100:2-3

Journal Questions

- Write about how the gift of Christian community has been a blessing to you.
- What kinds of Christian communities are you a part of?
- Do you have a spiritual friend, someone with whom you can speak about faith, confide in, who encourages you, guides you and, if needed, corrects you—and for whom you are the same? If so, reflect on that relationship and what it means to you. If not, could you build a friendship like that?

Intercession

Give thanks for all the Christian communities and friends (name them) who support you in your life of faith.

Prayer for Today

Lord, enable me to be a strength of my Christian communities, and faithful in my spiritual friendships.

Notes

Day 23

THERE IS PROBABLY NO CHRISTIAN to whom God has not given the uplifting and blissful *experience* of genuine Christian community at least once in her or his life. But in this world such experiences remain nothing but a gracious extra beyond the daily bread of Christian community life. We have no claim to such experiences, and we do not live with other Christians for the sake of gaining such experiences. It is not the experience of Christian community, but firm and certain faith within Christian community that holds us together. We hold fast in faith to God's greatest gift, that God has acted for us all and wants to act for us all. This makes us joyful and happy, but it also makes us ready to forget all such experiences if at times God does not grant them. We are bound together by faith, not by experience.

BIBLICAL WISDOM

Finally, all of you, have unity of spirit, sympathy, love for one another, a tender heart, and a humble mind. Do not repay evil for evil or abuse for abuse; but, on the contrary, repay with a blessing. It is for this that you were called—that you might inherit a blessing. 1 Peter 3:8-9

SILENCE FOR MEDITATION

QUESTIONS TO PONDER

- Why is "the uplifting and blissful *experience* of genuine Christian community" somewhat rare?
- What is the "firm and certain faith" that holds Christians together even when there is conflict and tension between them?
- What does it mean to say: "We are bound together by faith, not by experience"?

Psalm Fragment

How very good and pleasant it is
when kindred live together in unity!
It is like the precious oil on the head,
running down upon the beard,
on the beard of Aaron,
running down over the collar of his robes. Psalm 133:1-2

Journal Reflections

- Write about an "uplifting and blissful" experience of genuine Christian community in your life.
- Write about a time when faith kept you in community even though the *experience* of community wasn't so good at the time.

Intercessions

Think about your community of faith. If there is any conflict or tension in the community, pray that faith in the unity given by Christ would sustain the community as it seeks to resolve the conflict. If the members of your community of faith are presently at peace with one another, thank God for the *experience* of unity.

Prayer for Today

Lord, I need Christian community. Help me to be there for others in the same way I need others to be there for me.

Notes

Journey

Day 24

EVERY HUMAN IDEALIZED IMAGE THAT is brought into the Christian community is a hindrance to genuine community and must be broken up so that genuine community can survive. Those who love their dream of a Christian community more than the Christian community itself become destroyers of that Christian community even though their personal intentions may be ever so honest, earnest, and sacrificial…

Those who dream of this idealized community demand that it be fulfilled by God, by others, and by themselves. They enter the community of Christians with their demands, set up their own law, and judge one another and even God accordingly…

Because God already has laid the only foundation of our community, because God has united us in one body with other Christians in Jesus Christ long before we entered into common life with them, we enter into that life together with other Christians, not as those who make demands, but as those who thankfully receive. We thank God for what God has done for us. We thank God for giving us other Christians who live by God's call, forgiveness, and promise. We do not complain about what God does not give us; rather we are thankful for what God does give us daily.

*

BIBLICAL WISDOM

I therefore, the prisoner in the Lord, beg you to lead a life worthy of the calling to which you have been called, with all humility and gentleness, with patience, bearing with one another in love, making every effort to maintain the unity of the Spirit in the bond of peace. There is one body and one Spirit, just as you were called to the one hope of your calling, one Lord, one faith, one baptism, one God and Father of all, who is above all and through all and in all. Ephesians 4:1-6

SILENCE FOR MEDITATION

Questions to Ponder

- What does it mean to love the "dream of Christian community more than the community itself"?
- If "we enter community not as those who make demands, but as those who thankfully receive," what should our attitude and action toward the community be?
- Is it easier to "complain about what God does not give us" or to be "thankful for what God does give us"? Why?

Psalm Fragment

The Lord is my strength and my shield;
in him my heart trusts;
so I am helped, and my heart exults,
and with my song I give thanks to him.
The Lord is the strength of his people;
he is the saving refuge of his anointed.
O save your people, and bless your heritage;
be their shepherd, and carry them forever. Psalm 28:7-9

Journal Reflections

- Write about your response to Bonhoeffer's ideas about Christian community.
- Does reading Bonhoeffer on Christian community change the way you feel about your faith community? How? Or why not?
- Does it suggest any practical changes in the way you relate to your faith community? If so, what are they?

Intercessions

Think about your faith community and spiritual friends (name them) and thank God for the support you get from them in living your life of faith.

Prayer for Today

Lord Jesus, I will be as important to my spiritual community as my spiritual community is to me.

Notes

CHRISTIANS ARE PERSONS WHO NO longer seek their salvation, their deliverance, their justification in themselves, but in Jesus Christ alone. They know that God's Word in Jesus Christ pronounces them guilty, even when they feel nothing of their own guilt, and that God's Word in Jesus Christ pronounces them free and righteous even when they feel nothing of their own righteousness…

Because they daily hunger and thirst for righteousness, they long for the redeeming Word again and again. It can only come from the outside. In themselves they are destitute and dead. Help must come from the outside; and it has come and comes daily and anew in the Word of Jesus Christ, bringing us redemption, righteousness, innocence, and blessedness. But God put this Word into the mouth of human beings so that it may be passed on to others. When people are deeply affected by the Word, they tell it to other people. God has willed that we should seek and find God's living Word in the testimony of other Christians, in the mouths of human beings. Therefore, Christians need other Christians who speak God's Word to them. They need them again and again when they become uncertain and disheartened.

BIBLICAL WISDOM

Remember your leaders, those who spoke the word of God to you; consider the outcome of their way of life, and imitate their faith. Hebrews 13:7

SILENCE FOR MEDITATION

QUESTIONS TO PONDER

- Where do disciples go to satisfy their *daily* hunger and thirst for righteousness?
- If Christians find their salvation, deliverance, and justification not in themselves but in Jesus Christ, how should they use their resulting freedom?

- If God has put God's word into the "mouth of human beings," who is responsible to speak the word? Only pastors or church workers? Why?

Psalm Fragment

On the glorious splendor of your majesty,
*   and on your wondrous works, I will meditate.*
The might of your awesome deeds shall be proclaimed,
*   and I will declare your greatness.*
They shall celebrate the fame of your abundant goodness,
*   and shall sing aloud of your righteousness.* Psalm 145:5-7

Journal Reflections

- Write about specific Christians who have spoken a word from God to you when you needed it.
- Write about people to whom you have spoken God's word.

Intercessions

Think of someone you would like to be a spiritual friend with and ask God to help you build a mutually supportive spiritual relationship with him or her.

Prayer for Today

O Holy Spirit, send the people I need to bring me the word of God, and send the people I need to speak the word of God to.

Notes

WHOEVER CANNOT BE ALONE SHOULD *beware of community*. Such people will only do harm to themselves and to the community. Alone you stood before God when God called you. Alone you had to obey God's voice. Alone you had to take up your cross, struggle, and pray and alone you will die and give an account to God. You cannot avoid yourself, for it is precisely God who has singled you out. If you do not want to be alone, you are rejecting Christ's call to you, and you can have no part in the community of those who are called...

But the reverse is also true. *Whoever cannot stand being in community should beware of being alone.* You are called into the community of faith; the call was not meant for you alone. You carry your cross, you struggle, and you pray in the community of faith, the community of those who are called. You are not alone even when you die, and on the day of judgment you will be only one member of the great community of faith of Jesus Christ...

Whoever cannot be alone should beware of community. Whoever cannot stand being in community should beware of being alone.

BIBLICAL WISDOM

For as in one body we have many members, and not all the members have the same function, so we, who are many, are one body in Christ, and individually we are members one of another. Romans 12:4-5

SILENCE FOR MEDITATION

QUESTIONS TO PONDER

- Why do so many people in our society seem to fear being alone?
- Why do so many churches seem to be mere aggregates of individuals rather than true *communities* of faith?
- In what ways can a disciple establish a healthy balance between aloneness and community?

Psalm Fragment

Praise the LORD!
I will give thanks to the LORD with my whole heart,
*   in the company of the upright, in the congregation.*
Great are the works of the LORD,
*   studied by all who delight in them.* Psalm 111:1-2

Journal Reflections

- Write about times when you have intentionally been alone. How did it make you feel? What did you do? Did your aloneness have any impact on how you felt when you were with others again?
- Write about your experience in community. Do you feel an integral part of your community? Do you feel like you have a good balance between time in community and time alone?

Intercessions

If you know anyone who seems lonely, pray that they might discover true community. If you know anyone who seems afraid to be alone with themselves, pray that they might discover the joy of solitude, of being alone with God.

Prayer for Today

O Lord, when I am too much alone, help me seek community. When I am too dependent on the community, help me to set aside time to be alone.

Notes

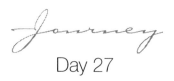

Day 27

(When Bonhoeffer speaks of community, he means any gathering of Christians, including the family.)

THE *FIRST* SERVICE ONE OWES to others in the community involves listening to them. Just as our love for God begins with listening to God's Word, the beginning of love for other Christians is learning to listen to them. … We do God's work for our brothers and sisters when we learn to listen to them. So often Christians, especially preachers, think that their only service is always to have to "offer" something when they are together with other people. They forget that listening can be a greater service than speaking. Many people seek a sympathetic ear and do not find it among Christians, because these Christians are talking even when they should be listening. But Christians who can no longer listen to one another will soon no longer be listening to God either; they will always be talking even in the presence of God.

BIBLICAL WISDOM
"Listen carefully to my words, and let my declaration be in your ears." Job 13:17

SILENCE FOR MEDITATION

QUESTIONS TO PONDER
- What do you think of Bonhoeffer's statement that "the beginning of love for other Christians is learning to listen to them"?
- In what way is listening to our brothers and sisters doing "God's work" for them?
- Why do you suppose so many people find it so difficult to listen?

PSALM FRAGMENT

But my people did not listen to my voice;
*   Israel would not submit to me.*
So I gave them over to their stubborn hearts,
*   to follow their own counsels.*
O that my people would listen to me,
*   that Israel would walk in my ways!* Psalm 81:11-13

JOURNAL REFLECTIONS

- Write about a time when you benefited from having another Christian listen to you.
- Write about your experience as a listener. Are you a good listener? Did you feel like you were doing God's work as you listened?

INTERCESSIONS

Think about someone in your community of faith who never seems listened to. Pray that they might have the courage to speak what is on their heart and mind, and pray that you would have the compassion and interest to listen to them.

PRAYER FOR TODAY

Lord Jesus, may I have the grace to listen to you and learn from you; may I have the grace to listen to and learn from others.

NOTES

Day 28

THE *OTHER* SERVICE ONE SHOULD perform for another person in a Christian community is active helpfulness. To begin with, we have in mind simple assistance in minor, external matters. There are many such things wherever people live together. Nobody is too good for the lowest service. Those who worry about the loss of time entailed by such small, external acts of helpfulness are usually taking their own work too seriously. We must be ready to allow ourselves to be interrupted by God, who will thwart our plans and frustrate our ways time and again, even daily, by sending people across our path with their demands and requests.

BIBLICAL WISDOM

"The greatest among you will be your servant." Matthew 23:11

SILENCE FOR MEDITATION

QUESTIONS TO PONDER

- What are the forms "active helpfulness" might take in a community of faith?
- Is it true that: "Nobody is too good for the lowest service"? Why, or why not?
- How does taking their own work too seriously tempt people to undervalue the real needs of others?

Psalm Fragment

For he [the ruler] delivers the needy when they call,
the poor and those who have no helper.
He has pity on the weak and the needy,
and saves the lives of the needy.
From oppression and violence he redeems their life;
and precious is their blood in his sight. Psalm 72:12-14

Journal Reflections

- Reflect on specific instances in which you were "interrupted by God" in the form of someone in need of help who crossed your path. What did you do? How did you feel about it?
- Write about your degree of willingness to be "interrupted by God."
- What might the "lowest service" be in your community of faith?

Intercession

Pray that your community of faith would be a place were God is free to interrupt anyone at any time for the sake of someone in any kind of need.

Prayer for Today

Lord, as I go about my business today, don't hesitate to interrupt me, and give me the grace to notice the interruption.

Notes

Day 29

THIRD, WE SPEAK OF THE service involved in bearing with others. "Bear one another's burdens, and in this way you will fulfill the law of Christ" (Gal. 6:2). Thus the law of Christ is a law of forbearance. Forbearance means enduring and suffering. The other person is a burden to the Christian, in fact for the Christian most of all. The other person never becomes a burden at all for the *pagans*. They simply stay clear of every burden the other person may create for them. However, Christians must bear the burden of one another. Only as a burden is the other really a brother or sister and not just an object to be controlled.

BIBLICAL WISDOM

So let us not grow weary in doing what is right, for we will reap at harvest time, if we do not give up. So then, whenever we have an opportunity, let us work for the good of all, and especially for those of the family of faith. Galatians 6:9-10

SILENCE FOR MEDITATION

QUESTIONS TO PONDER

- In what ways might "bearing with others" have a positive rather than negative connotation?
- What do you think of Bonhoeffer's assertion that: "The other person is a burden to the Christian"? Can that be a good way to look at other people?
- How does the church "bear with" the larger community that surrounds it?

Psalm Fragment

Cast your burden on the LORD,
*   and he will sustain you;*
*   he will never permit*
*   the righteous to be moved.* Psalm 55:22

Journal Reflections

- Think of the people in your life. To whom are you a burden? How does it feel?
- In what ways do the people in your life help bear your burdens?
- Whose burdens are you helping to bear? How does it feel?

Intercessions

Who in your circle of family, friends, and acquaintances is weighed down with heavy burdens? Pray for them in their need and ask God to show you how to help them bear those burdens.

Prayer for Today

Loving God, thank you for bearing with me; make me willing to bear with others.

Notes

Day 30

A CHRISTIAN COMMUNITY EITHER LIVES by the intercessory prayers of its members for one another, or the community will be destroyed. I can no longer condemn or hate other Christians for whom I pray, no matter how much trouble they cause me. In intercessory prayer the face that may have been strange and intolerable to me is transformed into the face of one for whom Christ died, the face of a pardoned sinner. That is a blessed discovery for the Christian who is beginning to offer intercessory prayer for others. As far as we are concerned, there is no dislike, no personal tension, no disunity or strife that cannot be overcome by intercessory prayer. Intercessory prayer is the purifying bath into which the individual and the community must enter every day.

BIBLICAL WISDOM

Pray in the Spirit at all times in every prayer and supplication. To that end keep alert and always persevere in supplication for all the saints. Ephesians 6:18

SILENCE FOR MEDITATION

QUESTIONS TO PONDER

- What is more common in the church, generic prayers for "those in need" or specific prayers for specific individuals? Why?
- How common is it for individual Christians and communities of faith to pray for the good of those they dislike or are in conflict with?
- In what ways does intercessory prayer protect a community of faith?

Psalm Fragment

Pray for the peace of Jerusalem:
"May they prosper who love you.
Peace be within your walls,
and security within your towers."
For the sake of my relatives and friends
I will say, "Peace be within you."
For the sake of the house of the Lord our God,
I will seek your good." Psalm 122:6-9

Journal Reflections

- Reflect on your prayer life. Have you ever prayed for the good of anyone you were in a conflict with?
- If so, what happened as a result of your prayer? Did it change the way you thought about that person?
- If not, reflect in your journal as to whether or not you are ready to pray for the good of people who have hurt you or whom you dislike for any reason.

Intercessions

Pray that your community of faith would be a place where conflict is resolved and hard feelings softened through intercessory prayer.

Prayer for Today

Forgiving God, may I see those with whom I am in conflict as your beloved, and may I share in your love for them by praying for them.

Notes

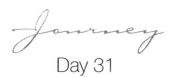

Day 31

OFFERING INTERCESSORY PRAYER MEANS NOTHING other than Christians bringing one another into the presence of God, seeing each other under the cross of Jesus as poor human beings and sinners in need of grace. Then, everything about other people that repels me falls away. Then I see them in all their need, hardship, and distress. Their need and their sin become so heavy and oppressive to me that I feel as if they were my own, and I can do nothing else but bid: Lord, you yourself, you alone, deal with them according to your firmness and your goodness.

BIBLICAL WISDOM

Therefore confess your sins to one another, and pray for one another, so that you may be healed. The prayer of the righteous is powerful and effective. James 5:15-16

SILENCE FOR MEDITATION

QUESTIONS TO PONDER

- How does seeing others under the cross of Jesus Christ cause all that "repels me" about them to fall away?
- In what way is everyone equal under the cross?
- How does looking at other people through the lens of God's mercy change our feelings about them and about ourselves?

PSALM FRAGMENT

May he judge your people with righteousness,
and your poor with justice.
May the mountains yield prosperity for the people,
and the hills, in righteousness.
May he defend the cause of the poor of the people,
give deliverance to the needy,
and crush the oppressor. Psalm 72:2-4

JOURNAL REFLECTIONS

• Make a list of the people whom you would like to bring into the presence of God today.
• Write a line or two describing the nature of your relationship with each of these people.

INTERCESSIONS

For each person listed in your journal today, pray: Lord, you yourself, you alone, deal with (name) according to your firmness and your goodness.

PRAYER FOR TODAY

Forgiving and transforming God, thank you that under the cross of Christ we all stand equally together under your love and mercy.

NOTES

Day 32

INTERCESSORY PRAYER IS ALSO A daily service Christians owe to God and one another. Those who deny their neighbors prayers of intercession deny them a service Christians are called to perform. Furthermore, it is clear that intercessory prayer is not something general and vague, but something very concrete. It is interested in specific persons and specific difficulties and therefore specific requests. The more concrete my intercessory prayer becomes the more promising it is...

All this proves that intercessory prayer is a gift of God's grace for every Christian community and for every Christian. Because God has made us such an immeasurably great offer here, we should accept it joyfully. The very time we give to intercession will turn out to be a daily source of new joy in God and in the Christian congregation.

BIBLICAL WISDOM

"Moreover, as for me, far be it from me that I should sin against the Lord by ceasing to pray for you." 1 Samuel 12:23

SILENCE FOR MEDITATION

QUESTIONS TO PONDER

- Is it a contradiction to say that intercessory prayer is both a "daily service Christians owe to God and one another" and "a gift of God's grace for every Christian community and for every Christian"? Why, or why not?
- Could the lack of joy evident in many Christians and in many Christian communities be a sign of a lack of specific, concrete, intercessory prayer? Explain.

Psalm Fragment

But let all who take refuge in you rejoice;
  let them ever sing for joy.
Spread your protection over them,
  so that those who love your name may exult in you. Psalm 5:11

Journal Reflections

• Write about how you feel when praying for others in your community of faith.
• Is intercessory prayer "a daily source of new joy in God and in the Christian congregation" for you? Why, or why not?

Intercessions

Pray that your community of faith in particular, and all communities of faith in general, would experience the joy in God and in each other that comes from the service of daily prayer on behalf of their members.

Prayer for Today

Holy God, thank you for the joy of bringing people into your presence this day and every day.

Notes

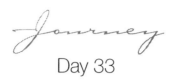

Day 33

EVERY ACT OF SELF-DISCIPLINE BY a Christian is also a service to the community. Conversely, there is no sin in thought, word, or deed, no matter how personal or secret, that does not harm the whole community. When the cause of an illness gets into one's body, whether or not anyone knows where it comes from, or in what member it has lodged, the body is made ill. This is the appropriate metaphor for the Christian community. Every member serves the whole body, contributing either to its health or to its ruin, for we *are* members of one body not only when we want to be, but in our whole existence. This is not a theory, but a spiritual reality that is often experienced in the Christian community with shocking clarity, sometimes destructively and sometimes beneficially.

BIBLICAL WISDOM

For as in one body we have many members, and not all the members have the same function, so we, who are many, are one body in Christ, and individually we are members one of another. Romans 12:4-5

SILENCE FOR MEDITATION

QUESTIONS TO PONDER

- What do you think Bonhoeffer means by an "act of self-discipline"?
- How can an individual's sins "harm the whole community"?
- What are the implications of Bonhoeffer's assertion that, "we *are* members of one body not only when we want to be, but in our whole existence"?

Psalm Fragment

Search me, O God, and know my heart;
  test me and know my thoughts.
See if there is any wicked way in me,
  and lead me in the way everlasting. Psalm 139:23-24

Journal Reflections

- Reflect on your experience in your community of faith. Does it feel like a living body of which you are a member? Explain.
- How might you better serve "the whole body"?

Intercession

If there is any "illness" in that expression of the "body of Christ" where you worship, pray for God's healing and transforming power.

Prayer for Today

Holy God, thank you that you have made me a member of the Body of Christ; help me keep healthy that I may not harm the whole body.

Notes

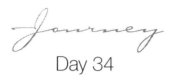

Day 34

OFTEN WE COMBAT OUR EVIL thoughts most effectively if we absolutely refuse to allow them to be verbalized. It is certain that the spirit of self-justification can only be overcome by the spirit of grace; and it is just as certain that the individual judgmental thought can be limited and suppressed by never allowing it to be spoken except as a confession of sin.... Thus it must be a decisive rule of all Christian community life that each individual is prohibited from talking about another Christian in secret. It is clear and will be shown in what follows that this prohibition does not include the word of admonition that is spoken personally to one another. However, talking about others in secret is not allowed even under the pretense of help and goodwill. For it is precisely in this guise that the spirit of hatred between believers always creeps in, seeking to cause trouble.

BIBLICAL WISDOM

Let no evil talk come out of your mouths, but only what is useful for building up, as there is need, so that your words may give grace to those who hear. Ephesians 4:29

SILENCE FOR MEDITATION

QUESTIONS TO PONDER

- Talking with people about someone else you are having trouble with when they are not there is called "triangulation." In what ways does triangulation harm a community of faith?
- How can a community of faith enforce the rule "that each individual is prohibited from talking about another Christian in secret"?
- Would this be a good rule to generalize and apply to the workplace, school, families, among friends? Why, or why not?

Psalm Fragment

Set a guard over my mouth, O Lord;
keep watch over the door of my lips.
Do not turn my heart to any evil,
to busy myself with wicked deeds
in company with those who work iniquity.... Psalm 141:3-4

Journal Reflections

- Have you ever experienced being triangulated—being talked about negatively when you where not there? If so, write about the experience. How did it feel?
- Have you ever engaged in triangulation? If so, write about the experience. How did it feel?

Intercession

If you are aware of triangulation in your community of faith, workplace, among family or friends, pray that those involved would receive the grace and courage to deal positively and directly with each other to resolve the conflict.

Prayer for Today

Spirit of love, may the words I speak be the kind that build people up.

Notes

THUS THERE REMAINS ONLY ONE path for those who in following Jesus want to truly serve God in worship, and that is the path of reconciliation with their sisters and brothers. Anyone who comes to the word and sacrament with an unreconciled heart stands judged by doing so. Such a person is a murderer in God's sight. That is why you must "first be reconciled to your brother or sister, and then come and offer your gift." It is a difficult path Jesus imposes on his disciples. It includes much humiliation and dishonor for the disciples themselves. But it is the path to him, our crucified brother, and thus, it is a path full of grace. In Jesus, service to the least brother or sister and service to God became one. He went and was reconciled to his human kindred, and then he came and offered himself, the one true sacrifice, to his Father.

BIBLICAL WISDOM

"So when you are offering your gift at the altar, if you remember that your brother or sister has something against you, leave your gift there before the altar and go; first be reconciled to your brother and sister, and then come and offer your gift."
Matthew 5:23-24

SILENCE FOR MEDITATION

QUESTIONS TO PONDER

- Bonhoeffer states that: "It is a difficult path Jesus imposes on his disciples." What makes it difficult?
- He also states that, "it is a path full of grace." Where is the grace?
- How did Jesus model the truth that, "service to the least brother or sister and service to God became one"?

Psalm Fragment

O guard my life, and deliver me;
*   do not let me be put to shame, for I take refuge in you.*
May integrity and uprightness preserve me,
*   for I wait for you.* Psalm 25:20-21

Journal Reflections

- Is there someone with whom you need to be reconciled? Write about the circumstances that led to alienation from this person.
- What step(s) might you take to begin the process of reconciliation?

Intercession

Pray for the person you wrote about in your journal, that they too might be open to and desirous of reconciliation. If there is no one with whom you personally need to seek reconciliation, pray for estranged people that you know, that they might find the way to reconciliation with each other.

Prayer for Today

Gracious God, thank you for reconciling me to yourself; now make me a reconciler.

Notes

Day 36

When another Christian falls into obvious sin, an admonition is imperative, because God's Word demands it. The practice of discipline in the community of faith begins with friends who are close to one another. Words of admonition and reproach must be risked when a lapse from God's Word in doctrine or life endangers a community that lives together, and with it the whole community of faith. Nothing can be more cruel than that leniency which abandons others to their sin. Nothing can be more compassionate than that severe reprimand which calls another Christian in one's community back from the path of sin. When we allow nothing but God's Word to stand between us, judging and helping, it is a service of mercy, an ultimate offer of genuine community. Then it is not we who are judging; God alone judges, and God's judgment is helpful and healing.

BIBLICAL WISDOM

My friends, if anyone is detected in a transgression, you who have received the Spirit should restore such a one in a spirit of gentleness. Galatians 6:1

SILENCE FOR MEDITATION

QUESTIONS TO PONDER

- Is sin taken seriously in today's church and by today's Christians? How is it, or how is it not?
- Why might it be "cruel" not to admonish someone whose behavior is obviously sinful? What are the dangers in admonishing someone?
- How might the church and individual Christians avoid being hypocritical and judgmental when admonishing a Christian brother or sister?

PSALM FRAGMENT

Restore us again, O God of our salvation,
and put away your indignation toward us. Psalm 85:4

JOURNAL REFLECTIONS

- Have you ever been admonished by another Christian? If so, write about the experience. How was it done? How did it feel? What were the results?
- Have you ever offered a word of admonition to another person? If so, write about the experience. How did it feel? What were the results?
- If you answered no to the above two questions, spend some time in writing reflecting upon the idea of taking sin seriously enough to admonish another and receive admonition from another.

INTERCESSION

Pray that in your community of faith everyone would be open to correcting one another when necessary *"in a spirit of gentleness."*

PRAYER FOR TODAY

Lord, open my ears that I may hear from your Word whatever words of admonition I need to hear that I might grow in love and faithfulness.

NOTES

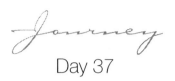

Day 37

(Bonhoeffer's view of a life among enemies was formed in the Nazi Germany of the 1930s, a situation that was becoming increasingly hostile to Christians.)

THE CHRISTIAN CANNOT SIMPLY TAKE for granted the privilege of living among other Christians. Jesus Christ lived in the midst of his enemies. In the end all his disciples abandoned him. On the cross he was all alone, surrounded by criminals and the jeering crowds. He had come for the express purpose of bringing peace to the enemies of God. Christians, too, belong not in the seclusion of a cloistered life but in the midst of enemies. There they find their mission, their work.

BIBLICAL WISDOM

"See, I am sending you out like sheep into the midst of wolves; so be wise as serpents and innocent as doves." Mathew 10:16

SILENCE FOR MEDITATION

QUESTIONS TO PONDER

- How would you define the "enemies" Christians are to live "in the midst of"?
- What is the "mission" or "work" of Christians toward these "enemies"?
- Jesus said: *"Love your enemies, do good to those who hate you, bless those who curse you, pray for those who abuse you"* (Luke 6:27-28). Does this fit with the reading from Bonhoeffer for today? How, or how not?

Psalm Fragment

You prepare a table before me
*   in the presence of my enemies;*
*   you anoint my head with oil;*
*   my cup overflows.*
Surely goodness and mercy shall follow me
*   all the days of my life,*
*   and I shall dwell in the house of the LORD*
*   my whole life long.* Psalm 23:5-6

Journal Reflections

- As a Christian, do you find yourself living "in the midst of enemies"? How, or how not? If so, who are they? How do you feel about them?
- What do you understand to be your personal mission or work in the midst of these enemies?

Intercession

Pray for all those whom you consider your "enemies," that God would bless them and that their lives would be good for themselves and for others.

Prayer for Today

Lord Jesus, give me the faith, the courage, and the love to live faithfully in the midst of enemies as you did.

Notes

Day 38

WORDS AND THOUGHTS ARE NOT enough. Doing good involves all the things of daily life. "If your enemies are hungry, feed them; if they are thirsty, give them something to drink" (Romans 12:20). In the same ways that brothers and sisters stand by each other in times of need, bind up each other's wounds, ease each other's pain, love of the enemy should do good to the enemy. Where in the world is there greater need, where are deeper wounds and pain than those of our enemies? Where is doing good more necessary and more blessed than for our enemies?

BIBLICAL WISDOM

"Love your enemies, do good to those who hate you, bless those who curse you, pray for those who abuse you." Luke 6:27-28

SILENCE FOR MEDITATION

QUESTIONS TO PONDER

- Does it seem counterintuitive to "do good to the enemy"? Why, or why not?
- Why should the needs of our enemies matter to us?
- What happens to the word "enemy" if we follow Bonhoeffer's advice and treat them like brothers and sisters?

Psalm Fragment

Your commandment makes me wiser than my enemies,
*   for it is always with me.* Psalm 119:98

Journal Reflections

- Does Jesus command to: *"Love your enemies, do good to those who hate you, bless those who curse you, pray for those who abuse you"* give you strength and vision for living in the midst of enemies? Why, or why not?
- Jesus teaching seems to call for non-violence in dealing with our enemies. Reflect in writing what you think about that.

Intercessions

Pray that your "enemies" might receive every good from the hand of God and in response become instruments of God's love and justice.

Prayer for Today

Holy God who loves us all with an everlasting love, let my love for my enemies be a matter not only of words or thoughts but of specific and concrete actions.

Notes

Journey

Day 39

IN PRAYER WE GO TO our enemies, to stand at their side. We are with them, near them, for them before God. Jesus does not promise us that the enemy we love, we bless, to whom we do good, will not abuse and persecute us. They will do so. But even in doing so, they cannot harm and conquer us if we take this last step to them in intercessory prayer. Now we are taking up their neediness and poverty, their being guilty and lost, and interceding for them before God. We are doing for them in vicarious representative action what they cannot do for themselves. Every insult from our enemy will only bind us closer to God and to our enemy. Every persecution can only serve to bring the enemy closer to reconciliation with God, to make love more unconquerable.

How does love become unconquerable? By never asking what the enemy is doing to it, and only asking what Jesus has done. Loving one's enemies leads disciples to the way of the cross and into communion with the crucified one.

BIBLICAL WISDOM

"Love your enemies and pray for those who persecute you." Matthew 5:44

SILENCE FOR MEDITATION

QUESTIONS TO PONDER

- Why should we—in intercessory prayer—do for our enemies what they cannot do for themselves? What can't they do for themselves?
- Where does one get the strength to love, bless, and do good to their enemies knowing that they will most likely be abused and persecuted in response?
- Why would Bonhoeffer say that: "Loving one's enemies leads disciples to the way of the cross and into communion with the crucified one"?

Psalm Fragment

In God, whose word I praise,
in the LORD, whose word I praise,
in God I trust; I am not afraid.
What can a mere mortal do to me?
My vows to you I must perform, O God;
I will render thank offerings to you.
For you have delivered my soul from death,
and my feet from falling,
so that I may walk before God
in the light of life. Psalm 56:10-13

Journal Reflections

- What emotions surface within you when you think of interceding on behalf of your enemies?
- Does your community of faith actively seek to love, bless, and do good for enemies? If so, how? If not, how could you encourage the practice?

Intercessions

Name your enemies, picture them in your mind, "stand at their side" before God, pray for them.

Prayer for Today

Lord of peace and justice, let me not so much want victory over my enemies as true and mutual reconciliation with them.

Notes

Day 40

Near the end of his life, Bonhoeffer was reported to have said the following:

WHAT BOTHERS ME INCESSANTLY IS the question…who Christ really is for us today?

⁔

BIBLICAL WISDOM

Now when Jesus came into the district of Caesarea Philippi, he asked his disciples, "Who do people say that the son of Man is?" and they said, "some say John the Baptist, but others Elijah, and still others Jeremiah or one of the prophets?" he said to them, "But who do you say that I am?" Simon Peter answered, "You are the messiah, the Son of the living God." Matthew 16:13-16

"Why do you call me 'Lord, Lord,' and do not do what I tell you? Luke 6:46

SILENCE FOR MEDITATION

QUESTIONS TO PONDER

- What is the relationship between who Jesus was two thousand years ago and "who Christ really is for us today"?
- Is there a difference between asking who Christ is for us and who Christ is for me? Explain.
- How do we go about answering the question about "who Christ really is for us today"?

Psalm Fragment

"Be still, and know that I am God!
I am exalted among the nations,
I am exalted in the earth." Psalm 46:10

Journal Reflections

- If someone asked you who Christ really is for you today, how would you answer?
- You have finished a *40-Day Journey with Dietrich Bonhoeffer*. How was the journey? What did you learn from Bonhoeffer? Has your understanding of what it means to be a Christian—to follow Jesus—changed? If so, how? What will be different in your life of faith for having taken this 40-day journey?

Intercessions

Pray for all those who will read this book, that their journey with Bonhoeffer might lead them closer to Christ.

Prayer for Today

Loving God, for where I have been and for where I am going on my journey with Jesus, I give you thanks and praise.

Notes

JOURNEY'S END

You have finished your *40-Day Journey with Dietrich Bonhoeffer*. I hope it has been a good journey and that along the way you have learned much and experienced much and found good resources to deepen your faith and practice. As a result of this journey:

- How are you different?
- What have you learned?
- What have you experienced?
- In what ways has your faith and practice been transformed?

NOTES

Do you want to continue the journey? If you would, there is a list of Bonhoeffer's books on the next page that will help you delve further into the thought, experience, and practice of this remarkable man.

For Further Reading

You can deepen your understanding of Dietrich Bonhoeffer and his work by reading his books. A good place to begin is with his books *Discipleship* and *Life Together.* Another small volume that is helpful is his *Psalms: The Prayer Book of the Bible.* After that you could follow your own interests. All of his books are being made available in a new English translation from Fortress Press.

To learn more about Bonhoeffer's life, you might want to begin with a short biography by his niece Renate Bethge, *Dietrich Bonhoeffer: A Brief Life* (Fortress, 2004). Also helpful is *Dietrich Bonhoeffer: A Life in Pictures,* edited by Renate Bethge and Christian Gremmels (Fortress, 2006). The definitive biography is by his friend and colleague Eberhard Bethge, *Dietrich Bonhoeffer: A Biography* (rev. ed., Fortress, 2000).

A very helpful resource is the website of the International Bonhoeffer Society: www.dbonhoeffer.org.

SOURCES

Dietrich Bonhoeffer. *Discipleship*, Dietrich Bonhoeffer Works, Vol. 4. Minneapolis: Fortress Press, 2001.

_____. *Life Together,* Dietrich Bonhoeffer Works, Vol. 5. Minneapolis: Fortress Press, 1996.

_____. *Letters and Papers from Prison.* New York: Collier Books, 1972.

Eberhard Bethge. *Dietrich Bonhoeffer: A Biography,* rev. ed. Minneapolis: Fortress Press, 2000.

Day 1: *Discipleship*, 39-40

Day 2: *Life Together,* 86-87

Day 3: *Life Together,* 76

Day 4: *Life Together,* 74-75

Day 5: *Life Together,* 37

Day 6: *Discipleship*, 163

Day 7: *Discipleship*, 165

Day 8: *Discipleship*, 102-3

Day 9: *Discipleship*, 104

Day 10: *Discipleship*, 105

Day 11: *Discipleship*, 106

Day 12: *Discipleship*, 106-7

Day 13: *Discipleship*, 107-8

Day 14: *Discipleship*, 108

Day 15: *Discipleship*, 108-9

Day 16: *Discipleship,* 111

Day 17: *Discipleship,* 43-44

Day 18: *Discipleship,* 55

Day 19: *Discipleship,* 44-45

Day 20: *Discipleship,* 64

Day 21: *Discipleship,* 66

Day 22: *Life Together,* 30

Day 23: *Life Together,* 47

Day 24: *Life Together,* 25

Day 25: *Life Together,* 33

Day 26: *Life Together,* 82-83

Day 27: *Life Together,* 98

Day 28: *Life Together,* 99

Day 29: *Life Together,* 100

Day 30: *Life Together,* 90

Day 31: *Life Together,* 90

Day 32: *Life Together,* 91

Day 33: *Life Together,* 92

Day 34: *Life Together,* 94

Day 35: *Discipleship,* 124

Day 36: *Life Together,* 105

Day 37: *Life Together,* 27

Day 38: *Discipleship,* 140

Day 39: *Discipleship,* 140-41

Day 40: *Dietrich Bonhoeffer: A Biography,* 863-64

We gratefully acknowledge the publishers who granted permission to reprint material from the following sources:

Dietrich Bonhoeffer Works, Volume 4: Copyright © 2001 Augsburg Fortress. All rights reserved. New *Dietrich Bonhoeffer Works* English-language translation of material first published as *The Cost of Discipleship:* Copyright © 1949, 1959, 2001 by Simon & Schuster Inc. and SCM-Canterbury Press Ltd. All rights reserved.

Life Together in Dietrich Bonhoeffer Works, Volume 5 by Dietrich Bonhoeffer, trans: Daniel W. Bloesch, ed. Geffrey B. Kelly. © 1996 HarperCollins, Publishers, Inc. All rights reserved.

NOTES

NOTES